MOTIVATIO

INSPIRATION FOR PRODUCTIVITY

Discover The Secrets To Getting
Things Done Ever Single Time
Without Fail

FLORES GREEN

Table of Contents

PART 1

Chapter 1:

The Goal Is Not The Point

If you ever want to achieve your goals, stop thinking about them. I know this goes against everything anyone has ever said about achieving your goals.

Everyone says that think about one thing and then stick to it. Devote yourself to that one single goal as you are committed to your next breath. Check on your goals over and over again to see if you are still on track or not and you will get there sooner than you think.

What I am proposing is against all the theories that exist behind achieving your goals but wait a minute and listen to me.

The reason behind this opposing theory is that we spend more time concentrating on thinking and panning about our goals. Rather than actually doing something to achieve them.

We think about getting into college. Getting a Bachelor's degree and then getting our Master's degree and so on. So that we can finally decide to appear for an interview that we have dreamed about or to start a business that we are crazy about.

But these are not the requirements for any of them to happen. You can get a degree in whatever discipline you want or not, and can still opt for business. As far as job interviews are concerned, they are not looking for the most educated person for that post. But the most talented and experienced person that suits the role on hand.

So we purposefully spend our life doing things that carry the least importance in actual to that goal.

What we should be doing is to get started with the simplest things and pile upon them as soon as possible. Because life is too short to keep thinking.

Thinking is the easiest way out of our miseries. Staying idol and fantasizing about things coming to reality is the lamest thing to do when you can actually go out and start discovering the opportunities that lie ahead of you.

Your goals are things that are out of your control. You might get them, you might not. But the actions, motivation, and the effort you put behind your goal make the goal a small thing when you actually grab it. Because then you look back and you feel proud of yourself for what you have achieved throughout the journey.

At the end of that journey, you feel happier and content with what you gained within yourself irrespective of the goal. Because you made yourself realize your true potential and your true purpose as an active human being.

Find purpose in the journey for you can't know for sure about what lies ahead. But what you do know is that you can do what you want to do to your own limits. When you come to realize your true potential, the original goal seems to fade away in the background. Because then your effort starts to appear in the foreground.

A goal isn't always meant to be achieved as it might not be good for you in the end or in some other circumstances. But the efforts behind these goals serve as something to look back on and be amazed at.

Chapter 2:
The Easiest Way to Live a Short,
Unimportant Life

An essential and successful life may seem intriguing but, sometimes it's just a lot of work. Whereas, in comparison, a short and unimportant life seems easier to live. The one reason for this may be that you need to eat up your surroundings. People who donate to this world live longer. So, you don't donate. You consume the world. But there is no doubt that people who live longer have many advantages, whereas someone living a short life would not have time for that. Not only is it a loss, but it will affect your life in which you are breathing already.

Few things can lead a person to an unimportant and unhealthy lifestyle. Of course, no one can control how many days we will live on this planet but, we can contribute to our surroundings. And even if you come up with small things, they can impact your life somehow. Be yourself when it comes to shaping. Don't let this world shape you but yourself. It may not only change your life but, it can also give them the confidence to others to change their lives.

It would help if you believed that you could live. If you give up on your life, life will give up on you. Keep yourself worth running in every factor of life. It would be best if you made yourself feel worth it to keep up with the world. Live a meaningful life by all means. How? By contributing to things, talk with a friend, take a long walk in the mornings, or call the people you care about. Even saying hi to a stranger count as contributing to this world. And small contribution leads towards a more significant source of the outcome.

Talk with yourself about how you are going to live this life, and live, not survive. Thet both are different things. We won't know if tomorrow will be our last day, so we got to live it today as it is. Nowadays, we tend to live our lives by ourselves. We prefer to talk on the phone instead of meeting up. It just leads towards an unhealthy and unimportant life. Meet up if you can. Contribute your ideas or decisions to that plan. Make sure that you work out your best if you want it to be done.

A short and unimportant life may seem easier to live by but, it's non-enjoyable. It's full of disadvantages and losses from every side. Isn't it better to live? To give it all your best? We need to devote most of ourselves to this one life that we got. And live each day to its fullest.

Chapter 3:
Structure Your Day With Tasks You Excel At and Enjoy

Today's video will probably appeal to people who have a say in the way they can structure their day. People who are working on their own businesses, or are freelancers. But it could also apply to those with full time jobs if your jobs allow flexibility.

For those who have been doing their own thing for a while, we know that it is not easy to put together a day that is truly enjoyable. We forget about doing the things we like and excel at, and start getting lost in a sea of work that we have to drag ourselves through doing.

If we don't have a choice, then I guess we can't really do anything about it. But if we do, we need to start identifying the tasks that require the most attention but the least effort on our part to do. Tasks that seem just about second-nature to us. Tasks that we would do even if nobody wanted to pay us. Tasks that allow our creativity to grow and expand, tasks that challenge us but not drain us, tasks that enriches us, or tasks that we simply enjoy doing.

The founding father of modern Singapore, one of the wealthiest countries in the world, Mr Lee Kuan Yew once said, find what works and just keep doing it over and over again. I would apply that to this situation as well. We have to find what works for us and just double down on it. The other stuff that we aren't good at, either hire someone else to do it, or find a way to do less of it or learn how to be good at it fast. Make it a challenge for ourselves. Who knows maybe you might find them enjoyable once you get a hang of it as well.

But for those things that already come naturally to us, do more of it. Pack a lot of time into at the start of the day. Dedicated a few hours of your day to those meaningful tasks that you excel at. You will find that once you get the creative juices and the momentum going, you will be able to conquer the other less pleasing tasks more easily knowing that you've already accomplished your goals for the day.

Start right now. Identify what those tasks that you absolutely love to do right now, work-wise, or whatever it may be, and just double down on it. Watch your day transform.

Wondering If You Have Chosen The Right Career Path

In today's topic we are going to touch on the subject of career once again. Because feeling there's nothing worse than feeling like you are not on the right path, that you are not meant to be where you are right now, that you feel regret for going down this road in the first place.

Hopefully by the end of this video I am able to shed some light into what being on the right career path really means, and that you are indeed on it as we speak.

For those of us who are lucky enough to have gone to get a formal degree in whatever universities in whatever countries, be it IVY league schools, or some neighbourhood universities, we tend to think the course that we have decided to major in will become the thing that we will do for the rest of our lives. But more often than not, for those of us who have had enough work experiences, we know that we don't always end up where we began in our work life.

Life is all about choices and decisions. But life never ever stays the same. When we go out into the real world, sometimes our expectations of a job doesn't match up with reality. And we only realise that after spending enough time pursuing that career path.

From many of my countless interviews and people that I've spoke to, almost all view their degree as a stepping stone to something else. Rarely does one person commit to pursuing their major for the rest of their lives. The only few exceptions being those that go to medical school or some other professional degree that they have invested maybe close to a decade mastering their field of study. The opportunity costs for these people are too high and many a times they stick to their careers because they have already invested too much and are in too deep to back out now.

For the vast majority of us, we tend not to have such a deep and emotional connection to our primary field of study that it is much easier for us to pursue something else if we are not happy. 3 to 4 years while it might sound painful to waste, it certainly doesnt sound as bad as 12 years of education in the medical field. 4 years pre med, 4 years medical school, and then maybe another 4 years residency. All those years truly add up. Not to mention all the school fees that had gone into that.

To answer the question about whether you have pursued the right career path, I believe that you are meant to be exactly where you are right now. Because only when you realise that you may not necessarily like your path, can you actually make the informed decision to do something about it like change job or pursue other fields of interest. Without this experience of the path you are on right now, you just never really know whether you would have regretted not even trying it in the first place.

As humans, it is in our DNA to explore. We love novel experiences, we love to see new things and places, we love to learn and grow. Without all these factors, we may end up feeling like we are actually dying. If we find that our career doesn't give us that satisfaction anymore. Hey It's absolutely okay to feel that way. That gives you the confidence to know that you might want to try something else instead and that maybe this isnt for you. Don't feel like you've wasted time because your skills will most definitely be transferable and another door will open for you should you be brave enough to turn the knob.

With this I challenge each and every one of you to stop asking yourself whether you are on the right career path and start believing that where you are right now is beautiful. That you are meant to be where you are right now and asking the questions that you need to be asking about whether you are happy at your job and if there are other things you might want to consider pursuing. Take the leap of faith and never be afraid to try new things.

I hope you learned something today. Take care and I'll see you in the next one.

Chapter 4:

The Difference Between Professionals and Amateurs

It doesn't matter what you are trying to become better at. If you only do the work when you're motivated, then you'll never be consistent enough to become a professional. The ability to show up every day, stick to the schedule, and do the work, especially when you don't feel like it — is so valuable that you need to become better 99% of the time. I've seen this in my own experiences. When I don't miss workouts, I get in the best shape of my life. When I write every week, I become a better writer. When I travel and take my camera out every day, I take better photos. It's simple and powerful. But why is it so difficult?

The Pain of Being A Pro

Approaching your goals — whatever they are — with the attitude of a professional isn't easy. Being a pro is painful. The simple fact of the matter is that most of the time, we are inconsistent. We all have goals that we would like to achieve and dreams that we would like to fulfill, but it doesn't matter what you are trying to become better at. If you only do the work when it's convenient or exciting, then you'll never be consistent enough to achieve remarkable results.

I can guarantee that if you manage to start a habit and keep sticking to it, there will be days when you feel like quitting. When you start a business, there will be days when you don't feel like showing up. When you're at the gym, there will be sets that you don't feel like finishing. When it's time to write, there will be days that you don't feel like typing. But stepping up when it's annoying or painful or draining to do so, that's what makes the difference between a professional and an amateur.

Professionals stick to the schedule. Amateurs let life get in the way. Professionals know what is important to them and work towards it with purpose. Amateurs get pulled off course by the urgencies of life. **You'll Never Regret Starting Important Work.**

Some people might think I'm promoting the benefits of being a workaholic. "Professionals work harder than everyone else, and that's why they're great." That's not it at all.

Being a pro is about having the discipline to commit to what is important to you instead of merely saying something is important to you. It's about starting when you feel like stopping, not because you want to work more, but because your goal is important enough to you that you don't simply work on it when it's convenient. Becoming a pro is about making your priorities a reality.

There have been many sets that I haven't felt like finishing, but I've never regretted doing the workout. There have been many articles I haven't felt like writing, but I've never regretted publishing on schedule. There have been many days I've felt like relaxing, but I've never regretted showing up and working on something important to me.

Becoming a pro doesn't mean you're a workaholic. It means that you're good at making time for what matters to you — especially when you don't feel like it — instead of playing the role of the victim and letting life happen to you.

Chapter 5:

How To Set Smart Goals

Setting your goals can be a tough choice. It's all about putting your priorities in such a way that you know what comes first for you. It's imperative to be goal-oriented to set positive goals for your present and future. You should be aware of your criteria for setting your goals. Make sure your plan is attainable in a proper time frame to get a good set of goals to be achieved in your time. You would need hard work and a good mindset for setting goals. Few components can help a person reach their destination. Control what you choose because it will eternally impact your life.

To set a goal to your priority, you need to know what exactly you want. In other words, be specific. Be specific in what matters to you and your goal. Make sure that you know your fair share of details about your idea, and then start working on it once you have set your mind to it. Get a clear vision of what your goal is. Get a clear idea of your objective. It is essential to give a specification to your plan to set it according to your needs.

Make sure you measure your goals. As in, calculate the profit or loss. Measure the risks you are taking and the benefits you can gain from them. In simple words, you need to quantify your goals to know what order to set them into. It makes you visualize the amount of time it will take or the energy to reach the finish line. That way, you can calculate your goals and their details. You need to set your mind on the positive technical growth of your goal. That is an essential step to take to put yourself to the next goal as soon as possible.

If you get your hopes high from the start, it may be possible that you will meet with disappointment along the way. So, it would be best if you made sure that your goals are realistic and achievable. Make sure your goal is within reach. That is the reality check you need to force in your mind that is your goal even attainable? Just make sure it is, and everything will go as planned. It doesn't mean to set small goals. There is a difference between big goals and unrealistic goals. Make sure to limit your romantic goals, or else you will never be satisfied with your achievement.

Be very serious when setting your goals, especially if they are long-term goals. They can impact your life in one way or another. It depends on you how you take it. Make sure your goals are relevant. So, that you can gain real benefit from your goals. Have your fair share of profits from your hard work and make it count. Always remember why the goal matters to you. Once you get the fundamental idea of why you need this goal to be achieved, you can look onto a bigger picture in the frame. If it doesn't feel relevant, then there is no reason for you to continue working for. Leave it as it is if it doesn't give you what you applied for because it will only drain your energy and won't give you a satisfactory outcome.

Time is an essential thing to keep in focus when working toward your goals. You don't want to keep working on one thing for too long or too short. So, keep a deadline. Keep a limit on when to work on your goal. If it's worth it, give it your good timer, but if not, then don't even waste a second on it. They are just some factors to set your goals for a better future. These visionary goals will help you get through most of the achievements you want to get done with.

Chapter 6:

The 5 Second Rule

Today I'm going to share with you a very special rule in life that has worked wonders for me ever since I discovered it. And that is known as the 5 second rule by Mel Robbins.

You see, on a daily basis, I struggle with motivation and getting things done. I struggle with the littlest things like replying an email, to responding to a work request. This struggle has become such a bad habit that before I think about beginning any sort of work, I would first turn on my Netflix account to watch an episode or two of my favourite sitcom, telling myself that I will get right on it after I satisfy this side of me first.

This habit of procrastination soon became so severe that I would actually sit and end up wasting 4-5 hours of time every morning before I would actually even begin on any work-related stuff. Before I knew it, it would be 3pm and I haven't gotten a single thing done. All the while I was staring at the clock, counting the number of hours I have wasted, while simultaneously addicted to procrastinating that I just could not for the life of me get myself off the couch onto my desk to begin any meaningful work.

I realized that something had to change. If I kept this up, I would not only not get anything done, like ever, but i would also begin to loathe myself for being so incredibly unproductive and useless. This process of self-loathing got worse everyday I leaned into the habit of procrastination. It was only until i stumbled onto Mel Robbin's 5 second rule that I started to see a real change in my habits.

The rule is simple, to count backwards from 5 and to just get up and go do that thing. It sounded stupid to me at first, but it worked. Instead of laying around in bed every morning checking my phone before I woke up, I would count backwards from 5 and as soon as it hit 1, i would get up and head straight towards the shower, or I would pack up my things and get out of my house.

I had identified that staying at home was the one factor that made me the most unproductive person on the planet, and that the only way I knew I was going to get real work done, was to get out of the house. I had also identified that showering was a good way to cleanse my mind from the night before. I really enjoyed showering as I always seem to have a clear head afterwards to be able to focus. What works for me, may not necessarily work for you. You have to identify for yourself when are the times you are most productive, and simply replicate it. A good way to find out is by journaling, which I will talk about in a separate video. Journaling is a good way to capture a moment in time and a particular state of mind. Try it for yourself the next time you are incredibly focused, write down how you got to that state, and simply do it again the next time to get there.

The 5 second rule is so simple yet so powerful because it snaps our unhealthy thought patterns. As Mel puts it, our brain is hardwired to protect us. We procrastinate out of fear of doing the things that are hard, so we have to beat our brain to it by disrupting it first. When we decide to move and take action after reaching 1, it is too late for our brains to stop us. And we get the ball rolling.

I was at my most productive on days that I felt my worst. But I overcame it because I didn't let my brain stop me from myself. I wouldn't say that I am struggle free now, but i knew i had a tool that would work most of the time to get me out of procrastination and into doing some serious work that would move my life forward. There are times when I would forget about the 5 second rule and my bad habits would kick in, but I always reminded myself that it was available to me if I chose to use it.

I would urge all of you who are struggling with any form of procrastination or laziness to give the 5 second rule a try. All you need to do is to get started and the rest becomes easy.

Chapter 7:

If You Commit to Nothing, You'll Be Distracted By Everything

I don't think anyone in their right mind would like to face a challenge where they have a chance to face failure or even a possibility of it.

We all need a new lesson to learn. A lesson of commitment and conviction. A lesson of integrity, grit, and sheer will. One might ask, why should I adopt the features of a soldier rather than a normal social being. Why do I need to go to extremes?

The answer to these questions is simple yet heavy, with a load most people avoid their whole life.

We all have somewhat similar goals. We all want to be in a better place in better shape. We all want wealth. We all want healthy stable relationships. We all want respect and a million other things.

Ask yourself this; Have you ever actually tried hard enough for any of this to happen. Have you ever tried to dig deep till you found your last breath? But it felt good because you had a good enough reason and passion to pursue?

The goals of life are a compulsion to have. We all must have something to strive for. Something worth fighting for. Something we can look back and be happy about.

But having a goal and committing to it are two different things.

One can have a goal and still not be motivated enough to do anything in their power to achieve that thing. No matter how the road takes turns.

We need to have the inspiration to drive us through the rough patches of life. To make us keep pushing even if we get squeezed within the incidents happening around us.

Don't take this the wrong way but you have to accept the fact that whatever you are feeling has nothing to do with what you want to achieve. Because what you want to achieve is something that your life depends on. The goals you set aren't some wishes or a feeling that your gut gives you. These goals are the requirements of life with which you can finally say lived a happy successful life. And this statement is the ultimate purpose of your life.

You were given this life because you had the energy to go for things that weren't easy, but you had the potential to achieve these. All you needed was a little commitment and Zero distractions.

The commitment you need isn't a feeling that goes and on and off like a switch. Rather a distinct key for the lock of your life.

So if you still think you will have days where you can try one more time, Let me be clear; You better start thinking about the future of your next generation. Because I don't think they'd have one.

You need to be committed enough to do anything that takes you closer and closer to your goals and nothing that wastes a second out of your life.

Because either you go all in or you walk the line and hedge your bets. The bet here being your life.

Chapter 8:

How To Worry Less

How many of you worry about little things that affect the way you go about your day? That when you're out with your friends having a good time or just carrying out your daily activities, when out of nowhere a sudden burst of sadness enters your heart and mind and immediately you start to think about the worries and troubles you are facing. It is like you're fighting to stay positive and just enjoy your day but your mind just won't let you. It becomes a tug of war or a battle to see who wins?

How many of you also lose sleep because your mind starts racing at bedtime and you're flooded with sad feelings of uncertainty, despair, worthlessness or other negative emotions that when you wake up, that feeling of dread immediately overwhelms you and you just feel like life is too difficult and you just dont want to get out of bed.

Well If you have felt those things or are feeling those things right now, I want to tell you you're not alone. Because I too struggle with those feelings or emotions on a regular basis.

At the time of writing this, I was faced with many uncertainties in life. My business had just ran into some problems, my stocks weren't doing well, I had lost money, my bank account was telling me I wasn't good enough, but most importantly, i had lost confidence. I had lost the ability to face each day with confidence that things will get better. I felt that i was worthless and that bad things will always happen to me. I kept seeing the negative side of things and it took a great deal of emotional toll on me. It wasn't like i chose to think and feel these things, but they just came into my mind whenever they liked. It was like a parasite feeding off my negative energy and thriving on it, and weakening me at the same time.

Now your struggles may be different. You may have a totally different set of circumstances and struggles that you're facing, but the underlying issue is the same. We all go through times of despair, worry, frustration, and uncertainty. And it's totally normal and we shouldn't feel ashamed of it but to accept that it is a part of life and part of our reality.

But there are things we can do to minimise these worries and to shift to a healthier thought pattern that increases our ability to fight off these negative emotions.

I want to give you 5 actionable steps that you can take to worry less and be happier. And these steps are interlinked that can be carried out in fluid succession for the greatest benefit to you. But of course you can choose whichever ones speaks the most to you and it is more important that you are able to practice any one of these steps consistently rather than doing all 5 of them haphazardly. But I want to make sure I give you all the tools so that you can make the best decisions for yourself.

Try this with me right now as I go through these 5 steps and experience the benefit for yourself instead of waiting until something bad happens.

The very first step is simple. Just breathe. When a terrible feeling of sadness rushes into your body out of nowhere, take that as a cue to close your eyes, stop whatever you are doing, and take 5 deep breathes through your nose. Breathing into your chest and diaphragm. Deep breathing has the physiological benefit of calming your nerves and releasing tension in the body and it is a quick way to block out your negative thoughts. Pause the video if you need to do practice your deep breathing before we move on.

And as you deep breathe, begin the second step. Which is to practice gratefulness. Be grateful for what you already have instead of what you think u need to have to be happy. You could be grateful for your dog, your family, your friends, and whatever means the most to you. And if you cannot think of anything to be grateful for, just be grateful that you are even alive and walking on this earth today because that is special and amazing in its own right.

Next is to practice love and kindness to yourself. You are too special and too important to be so cruel to yourself. You deserve to be loved and you owe it to yourself to be kind and forgiving. Life is tough as it is, don't make it harder. If you don't believe in yourself, I believe in you and I believe in your worthiness as a person that you have a lot left to give.

The fourth step is to Live Everyday as if it were your last. Ask yourself, will you still want to spend your time worrying about things out of your control if it was your last day on earth? Will you be able to forgive yourself if you spent 23 out of the last 24 hours of your life worrying? Or will you choose to make the most out of the day by doing things that are meaningful and to practice love to your family, friends, and yourself?

Finally, I just want you to believe in yourself and Have hope that whatever actions you are taking now will bear fruition in the future. That they will not be in vain. That at the end of the day, you have done everything to the very best of your ability and you will have no regrets and you have left no stone unturned.

How do you feel now? Do you feel that it has helped at least a little or even a lot in shaping how you view things now? That you can shift your perspective and focus on the positives instead of the worries?

If it has worked for you today, I want to challenge you to consistently practice as many of these 5 steps throughout your daily lives every single day. When you feel a deep sadness coming over you, come back to this video if you need guidance, or practice these steps if you remember them on your own.

I wish you only good things and I hope that I have helped you that much more today. Thank you for your supporting me and this channel and if you find that I can do more for you, do subscribe to my channel and I'll see you in the next one. Take care.

Chapter 9:

How to Stop Chasing New Goals All the Time

The philosopher Alan Watts always said that life is like a song, and the sole purpose of the song is to dance. He said that when we listen to a song, we don't dance to get to the end of the music. We dance to enjoy it. This isn't always how we live our lives. Instead, we rush through our moments, thinking there's always something better, there's always some goal we need to achieve.

"Existence is meant to be fun. It doesn't go anywhere; it just is." Our lives are not about things and status. Even though we've made ourselves miserable with wanting, we already have everything we need. Life is meant to be lived. If you can't quit your job tomorrow, enjoy where you are. Focus on the best parts of every day. Believe that everything you do has a purpose and a place in the world.

Happiness comes from gratitude. You're alive, you have people to miss when you go to work, and you get to see them smile every day. We all have to do things we don't want to do; we have to survive. When you find yourself working for things that don't matter, like a big house or a fancy car, when you could be living, you've missed the point. You're playing the song, but you're not dancing.

"A song isn't just the ending. It's not just the goal of finishing the song. The song is an experience."

We all think that everything should be amazing when we're at the top, but it's not. Your children have grown older, and you don't remember the little things.

"...tomorrow and plans for tomorrow can have no significance at all unless you are in full contact with the reality of the present since it is in the present and only in the present that you live."

You feel cheated of your time, cheated by time. Now you have to make up for it. You have to live, make the most of what you have left. So you set another goal.

This time you'll build memories and see places, do things you never got the chance to do. The list grows, and you wonder how you'll get it all done and still make your large mortgage payment. You work more hours so you can do all this stuff "someday." You've overwhelmed yourself again.

You're missing the point.

Stop wanting more, <u>be grateful for</u> today. Live in the moment. Cherish your life and the time you have in this world. If it happens, it happens. If it doesn't, then it wasn't meant to; let it go.

"We think if we don't interfere, it won't happen."

There's always an expectation, always something that has to get done. You pushed aside living so that you could live up to an expectation that doesn't exist to anyone but you. The expectation is always there because you gave it power. To live, you've got to let it go.

You save all your money so that you can retire. You live to retire. Then you get old, and you're too tired to live up to the expectation you had of retirement; you never realize your dreams.

At forty, you felt cheated; at eighty, you are cheated. You cheated yourself the whole way through to the end.

"Your purpose was to dance until the end, but you were so focused on the end that you forgot to dance."

Chapter 10:

Six Steps To Create A Vision For Your Life

Hi everyone, for today's video, we are going to talk about how to create life's visions. You might be thinking, "why do we need to make these visions?" or "what are these visions for?".

Let me ask you this question, have you ever felt so stuck in where you are? That feeling when you wanna move and be somewhere else because you don't like where you are but you don't know where to go either? That is the worst feeling ever, right?

Creating a vision for your life will save you from being stuck and lost. These visions are the pictures you create about the life that you want to live.

Here are 6 Steps To Start Envisioning Your Future

Step number 1, identify what matters to you. Ask yourself, "what's really important to me?". Is it health? Career? Wealth? Relationships? Passion? Time? It could be a balance of all those things. What legacy would you want to leave in this world? Identifying what truly matters to you and what you really value gives you a destination of where you want to be. Having these in mind, all your plans and decisions will be centered towards your destination.

Next step is thinking ahead, but at the same time, also believing that it is already happening for you right now. Be specific in chasing what you want, don't just simply limit yourself to what you think is socially acceptable. If you limit your choices to what seems to be reasonable, you are disconnecting yourself from your true potentialDon't compromise.. Be as audacious as you want to be, it's your own life anyway! You have all the right to dream as big as you want. Talk as if your dreams are happening right now. When you have this big dream, you won't settle for less just because it is what's available at the moment.

Step number 3, assess and challenge your motives. Ask yourself, "is this the kind of life I wanna live because it is what the society is expecting from me?", "am I doing this because this is what everybody else is doing?" Knowing your real motive towards your visions will help you uncover what your heart really desires. You might even be surprised by what you'll discover within you when you remove all the layers that the world has planted in you.

Next step, be sure that your visions are aligned with a purpose. You don't need to know exactly what your life purpose is, unless you've already figured that out somehow. But your visions should be relevant to how you want your life to be. For example, if your goal is to maintain your mental well-being, your vision might be to live your life peacefully while focusing on the things that truly matter. Your vision should serve you the purpose into making your life as pleasing as you want it.

Step number 5 is to be accountable for your own visions. Don't tie your visions into someone else's hands. Your visions may involve direct impact to others but make sure that your visions are not dependent on other people. Why? Because people, just like the seasons, change. People come and go. The version of the people in your life right now is not how they will be for the rest of their lives. And so are you. Hold these visions in your own hands and make sure you execute it diligently and faithfully.

Last step is to make room for changes. You will grow as a person, that is a fact. You won't have the same exact priorities all through your life. And that's okay. Whatever you want to change into is valid. Your goals and dreams are all valid. Changes are inevitable so don't be afraid if you have to change what's working for you from time to time.

While you are in the process of making your life's visions, be as creative as you can. Although the world is not a wish-granting factory, remember that through your hard work and perseverance, nothing is really impossible. You have everything in you to achieve your goals and live through your visions. You just need to be clear about what you really want or where you wanna be.

Remember that our days in this world are limited. We won't be able to live our lives to the fullest if we are just merely existing or living by default. We are humans. And as humans, we have the power to lead the life we truly desire. Sometimes, we are just one decision away from it.

I hope what we've talked about today will not just inspire you to make your life's visions but also help you to understand why you need to make them. You deserve a kind of life that will excite you to wake up everyday because you know what you are waking up for.

That's all for today's video. Please don't forget to like and subscribe. I'll see you on the next one!

PART 2

Chapter 1:

How To Find Motivation

Today we're going to talk about a topic that hopefully will help you find the strength and energy to do the work that you've told yourself you've wanted or needed to but always struggle to find the one thing that enables you to get started and keep going. We are going to help you find motivation.

In this video, I am going to break down the type of tasks that require motivation into 2 distinct categories. Health and fitness, and work. As I believe that these are the areas where most of you struggle to stay motivated. With regards to family, relationships, and other areas, i dont think motivation is a real problem there.

For all of you who are struggling to motivate yourself to do things you've been putting off, for example getting fit, going to the gym, motivation to stay on a diet, to keep working hard on that project, to study for your exams, to do the chores, or to keep working on your dreams... All these difficult things require a huge amount of energy from us day in and day out to be consistent and to do the work.

I know... it can be incredibly difficult. Having experienced these ups and downs in my own struggle with motivation, it always starts off swimmingly... When we set a new year's resolution, it is always easy to think that we will stick to our goal in the beginning. We are super motivated to go do the gym to lose those pounds, and we go every single day for about a week... only to give up shortly after because we either don't see results, or we just find it too difficult to keep up with the regime.

Same goes for starting a new diet... We commit to doing these things for about a week, but realize that we just simply don't like the process and we give up as well...

Finding motivation to study for an important exam or working hard on work projects are a different kind of animal. As these are things that have a deadline. A sense of urgency that if we do not achieve our desired result, we might fail or get fired from our company. With these types of tasks, most of us are driven by fear, and fear becomes our motivator... which is also not healthy for us as stress hormones builds within us as we operate that way, and we our health pays for it.

Let's start with tackling the first set of tasks that requires motivation. And i would classify this at the health and fitness level. Dieting, exercise, going to the gym, eating healthily, paying attention to your sleep... All these things are very important, but not necessarily urgent to many of us. The deadline we set for ourselves to achieve these health goals are arbitrary. Based on the images we see of models, or people who seem pretty fit around us, we set an unrealistic deadline for ourselves to achieve those body goals. But more often than not, body changes don't happen in days or weeks for most of us by the way we train. It could take up to months or years... For those celebrities and fitness models you see on Instagram or movies, they train almost all day by personal trainers. And their deadline is to look good by the start of shooting for the movie. For most of us who have day jobs, or don't train as hard, it is unrealistic to expect we can achieve that body in the same amount of time. If we only set aside 1 hour a day to exercise, while we may get gradually fitter, we shouldn't expect that amazing transformation to happen so quickly. It is why so many of us set ourselves up for failure.

To truly be motivated to keep to your health and fitness goals, we need to first define the reasons WHY we even want to achieve these results in the first place. Is it to prove to yourself that you have discipline? Is it to look good for your wedding photoshoot? Is it for long term health and fitness? Is it so that you don't end up like your relatives who passed too soon because of their poor health choices? Is it to make yourself more attractive so that you can find a man or woman in your life? Or is it just so that you can live a long and healthy life, free of medical complications that plague most seniors by the time they hit their 60s and 70s? What are YOUR reasons WHY you want to keep fit? Only after you know these reasons, will you be able to truly set a realistic deadline for your health goals. For those that are in it for a better health overall until their ripe old age, you will realize that this health goal is a life long thing. That you need to treat it as a journey that will take years and decades. And small changes each day will add up. Your motivator is not to go to the gym 10 hours a day for a week, but to eat healthily consistently and exercise regularly every single day so that you will still look and feel good 10, 20, 30, 50 years, down the road.

And for those that need an additional boost to motivate you to keep the course, I want you to find an accountability partner. A friend that will keep you in check. And hopefully a friend that also has the same health and fitness goals as you do. Having this person will help remind you not to let yourself and this person down. Their presence will hopefully motivate you to not let your guard down, and their honesty in pointing out that you've been slacking will keep you in check constantly that you will do as you say.

And if you still require an additional boost on top of that, I suggest you print and paste a photo of the body that you want to achieve and the idol that you wish to emulate in terms of having a good health and fitness on a board where you can see every single day. And write down your reasons why beside it. That way, you will be motivated everytime you walk past this board to keep to your goals always.

Now lets move on to study and work related tasks. For those with a fixed 9-5 job and deadlines for projects and school related work, your primary motivator right now is fear. Which as we established earlier, is not exactly healthy. What we want to do now is to change these into more positive motivators. Instead of thinking of the consequences of not doing the task, think of the rewards you would get if you completed it early. Think of the relief you will feel knowing that you had not put off the work until the last minute. And think of the benefits that you will gain... less stress, more time for play, more time with your family, less worry that you have to cram all the work at the last possible minute, and think of the good results you will get, the opportunities that you will have seized, not feeling guilty about procrastinations... and any other good stuff that you can think of. You could also reward yourself with a treat or two for completing the task early. For example buying your favourite food, dessert, or even gadgets. All these will be positive motivators that will help you get the ball moving quicker so that you can get to those rewards sooner. Because who likes to wait to have fun anyway?

Now I will move on to talk to those who maybe do not have a deadline set by a boss or teacher, but have decided to embark on a new journey by themselves. Whether it be starting a new business, getting your accounting done, starting a new part time venture.. For many of these tasks, the only motivator is yourself. There is no one breathing down your neck to get the job done fast and that could be a problem in itself. What should we do in that situation? I believe with this, it is similar to how we motivate ourselves in the heath and fitness goals. You see, sheer force doesn't always work sometimes. We need to establish the reasons why we want to get all these things done early in life. Would it be to fulfil a dream that we always had since we were a kid? Would it be to earn an extra side income to travel the world? Would it be to prove to yourself that you can have multiple streams of income? Would it to become an accomplished professional in a new field? Only you can define your reasons WHY you want to even begin and stay on this new path in the first place. So only you can determine why and how you can stay on the course to eventually achieve it in the end.

Similarly for those of you who need additional help, I would highly recommend you to get an accountability partner. Find someone who is in similar shoes as you are, whether you are an entrepreneur, or self-employed, or freelance, find someone who can keep you in check, who knows exactly what you are going through, and you can be each other's pillars of support when one of you finds yourself down and out. Or needs a little pick me up. There is a strong motivator there for you to keep you on course during the rough time.

And similar to health and fitness goal, find an image on the web that resonates with the goal you are trying to achieve. Whether it might be to buy a new house, or to become successful, i want that image to always be available to you to look at every single day. That you never forget WHY you began the journey. This constant reminder should light a fire in you each and everyday to get you out of your mental block and to motivate you to take action consistently every single day.

So I challenge each and every one of you to find motivation in your own unique way. Every one of you have a different story to tell, are on different paths, and no two motivators for a person are the same. Go find that one thing that would ignite a fire on your bottom everytime you look at it. Never forget the dream and keep staying the course until you reach the summit.

Chapter 2:

Persistence

Today we're going to talk about persistency and how you can achieve success in your career and work life with it should you decide to make it a part of your identity.

So what is persistence and why is it important? Well to simply put, it is the act of not giving up, and not taking no for an answer. It is the act of having a thick skin, and a strong belief that you believe you have something great to offer and that it would be the loss of the person you are trying to woo over should they not take u up on it. It is a belief that despite the rejections you have been handed, you will not take it lying down, you will not give up, and you will try and try again until you receive a yes.

I believe that persistence is something that many of us lack, including myself. Many times when faced with a rejection, we feel a sense of dread and we start to question whether what we have to offer is indeed good enough. We start to doubt our self-worth and after maybe the 3rd or 4th rejection, we give up and we settle for something less than what we believe we should be worth.

True breakthroughs only come when we start to accept that rejections and people saying no to us is simply part of the game. It is a rite of passage. Because you can only get to a yes after you have received a few NOs along the way. Or if you're lucky, you may even get a yes on your first try. When we view rejection as a part of the process, we no longer have to fear it. And with persistence, we will find our way to a YES. And when we finally get it, even if it takes a thousand tries, it will all be worth it in the end.

We can also use rejections as a learning opportunity to see why we have gotten a NO and maybe to work on ourselves or our craft to stand out from the crowd the next time we present our offer to someone. Sometimes a no is simply a not right now, because maybe we lack certain qualifications or work experience, or uniqueness that we need to go find before coming back. We should not take rejection as a reflection on your character. By rather a growth opportunity.

Taylor Swift is a perfect example of how persistence paid off in the end. At 12 or 13, with a thick skin she went to record label after label in Nashville, and after receiving a few rejections, she realized that she needed to be different to clinch a record deal. Then she went home, and a smart girl she was at such a young age, she knew that a way she could stand out from the crowd was to pick up guitar and write her own songs. And with that persistence and determination to succeed, she got her yes from Big Machine Records and the rest is history.

This story of success is not unique to her. Famously Jack Ma was rejected probably about a thousand times until he founded Alibaba, and as we all know he is the head of an E-commerce empire in China. He believed in his vision and even without much charisma and good looks, he succeeded beyond the highest measure.

With these two powerful stories in mind, I challenge each of you today to believe in yourself and to have persistence in everything that you do. To take rejections as either a not-right-now, or a learning opportunity to grow before coming back stronger than ever. I believe every single one of you have to power to succeed in life and i wish you all the best in your endeavours. Take care and i'll see you in the next one.

Chapter 3:

Why You're Demotivated By A Values Conflict

Every human being, in fact, every organism in this universe is different from even the same member of their species. Every one of us has different traits, likes, dislikes, colors, smells, interests so it's natural to have a difference of opinion.

It's natural to have a different point of view. It's natural and normal to have a different way of understanding. And it's definitely normal for someone else to disagree with your ways of dealing with things.

Most of us don't want to see someone disagreeing with us because we have this tricky little fellow inside of us that we call EGO.

Our ego makes us feel disappointed when we see or hear someone doing or saying something better than us. We cannot let go of the fact that someone might be right or that someone might be Okay with being wrong and we can't do a single thing about it.

This conflict of values occurs within ourselves as well. We want to do one thing but we cannot leave the other thing as well. We want to have something but we cannot keep it just because we don't have the resources to maintain them.

This feeling of 'want to have but cannot have' makes us susceptible to feelings of incompleteness ultimately making us depressed. The reality of life is that you can't always get what you want. But that doesn't make it a good enough reason to give up on your dreams or stop thinking about other things too.

Life has a lot to offer to us. So what if you can't have this one thing you wanted the most. Maybe it wasn't meant for you in the first place. Nature has a way of giving you blessings even when you feel like you have nothing.

Let's say you want something but your mind tells you that you can't have it. So what you should do is to find alternative ways to go around your original process of achieving that thing and wait for new results. What you should do is to give up on the idea altogether just because you have a conflict within your personality.

You cannot let this conflict that is building within you get a hold of you. Clear your mind, remove all doubts, get rid of all your fears of failure or rejection, and start working from a new angle with a new perspective. Set new goals and new gains from the same thing you wanted the first time. This time you might get it just because you already thought you had nothing to lose.

This feeling of 'No Regret' will eventually help you get over any situation you ever come across after a fight with your inner self. This feeling can help you flourish in any environment no matter what other people say or do behind your back.

Nothing can bring you peace but yourself. Nothing holds you back but your other half within you.

Chapter 4:
How To Crush Your Goals This Quarter

Some people find it very hard to achieve their goals, but luckily, there is a method waiting to be used. The quarter method divides the year into four parts of 90-days; for each part, you set some goals to crush. The rest of the year has gone, and so have the three quarters; now it is time to prepare for the fourth quarter. 1st October is one of the most critical days in the life of a person who sets his goals according to the quarter. It is the benchmark representing the close of the third quarter and the beginning of the fourth quarter. It is the day when you set new goals for the upcoming three months; if somehow your third-quarter dreams were not crushed, then you can stage a comeback so you wouldn't be left behind forever. But how to achieve your fourth-quarter goals?

1st October may bring the start of a quarter, but it also ends another quarter; it is the day when you focus on your results. Have you achieved the goals you set for the third quarter? If not, then prepare yourself to hear the hard truth. Your results reflect your self-esteem; if you believe in yourself, then you would achieve your goals. If you are not satisfied with your results, think, is this what you had in mind? If no, then having small visions can never lead to a more significant impact. Limiting beliefs will never give you more than minor and unimpressive results. Your results tell you about your passion for your work; if you are not passionate about your work, you would have poor outcomes. We all have heard the famous saying, " work in silence and let your success make the noise," but what does this mean? It means that your results will tell everyone about your hard work. If your results are not satisfactory, you know that the problem is your behavior towards your work.

When setting goals for the future, one needs to accept the facts; what went wrong that put you off the track? The year is 75% complete, and if you still haven't crushed your goals, you need to accept that it is your fault. If you blame these failures on your upbringing, your education, or any other factor than yourself, then you are simply fooling yourself because it is all dependent on you. When you don't achieve what you wanted to in nine months, you must have figured the problem; it can be any bad habit you are not willing to give up or the strategies you are implying. If you pretend your habits, attitude, and approach are just fine, you are just fooling yourself, not anyone else. This benchmark is the best time to change the old bad habits and try forming some new strategies.

To finish the year with solid results, you need to get serious; the days of dissatisfied results are gone, now it is time to shine some light on your soul and determine what you are doing wrong, what habits are working in your favor, and which ones are not. Then you can decide which habits to give up on, which habits to improve, and which ones to keep. Once you have sorted this out, prioritize your goals and set some challenging destinations to avoid getting bored or feeling uninterested. When setting deadlines, try to set enforceable deadlines.

Confusion can lead to poor results, so sit back and think about the goals that I should not pursue. This is called understanding goal competition; the goals you set are competing for your time. Actual peak performance comes from understanding which goals to pursue and which not to seek. And when you complete a plan, don't just rush into the process of crushing the next goal; allow yourself to celebrate your win and feel the happiness of the goal finally getting destroyed by you.

Chapter 5:

How To Live In The Moment

Today we're going to talk about a different topic related to living in the moment. And this one has to do with those going through a health crisis or has a loved one who is going through one.

I hope that by the end of this video, that I will be able to encourage all of you to look at your life differently and look at how you treat your loved one who is going through a health issue with renewed eyes and perspective. Some of these concepts I derived from inspirational figures who have taught me some valuable lessons as well with their strength and resilience.

I know health can be a touchy subject. But i believe that it is something that we all struggle with at some point in our lives. When we are faced with a health scare or crisis, we will suddenly become aware of our own mortality and how fragile our lives really are. And then we start to worry about what might happen and what could happen if this and this occurs, if my health deteoriates, what that will look like, and we start scaring ourselves to no end and we start living our lives in fear that doing simple things become such a challenge for us.

I have had my fair share of health challenges. And I start worrying about the possible degradation of my body, of getting weaker, or getting old, or whatever, and get stuck in this mindset of worry. And we all know that we must not live our lives in fear, because fear is something we cannot really control. And what might happen to us is also not within our control.

What we can control however, when faced with a reality check in a health crisis, is to take stock once again of our life, the choices that we have made, health wise, eating the right foods, getting enough rest, and start fixing those things. Those are the things we can control. Another thing that is fully within our control, is to remember to live our lives in the present. When we realize time is not infinite, we need to remember to treasure each day without fear, and to start doing things now today that we won't regret. To start appreciating each day, savoring every sunset and sunrise, spending time with friends and family, and to never let ourselves get complacent with that. That we don't need multiple health scares in our lives to be reminded to live in the present and to life for the things that matter. You can't bring money with you when you die, but you can bring all your wonderful experiences at the end of your life and tell yourself that it is a life worth living. That is just me reminding u of what it might be like at the end of everyone's life, which is inevitable, this has got nothing to do with your health crisis that you are facing. I just want to be clear on that.

Another very very important thing that we need to be aware of is how we view our loved ones who are going through their own health crisis. If they have been diagnosed with something serious, and that time is of the essence, we need to show support to them by going through life with them to the fullest by spending time with them each and every day in the present moment. Live in the present with them and not worry about what could possibly happen to them. That this very second is magical with them and in this second they are alive and well. Who knows when their health could turn for the worst, and it doesn't really matter. They could live a longer life than you think. But the reality is that we never really know. And we should just cherish the present. I was inspired by this girl who suffered a terminal illness, Claire Wineland. She lived in such bravery and wisdom that she reminded everyone around her including her mom and myself, that in this moment, life is beautiful. That in this moment, life is amazing. And that in this moment, you are amazing.

So i just want to leave it as that. I hope you have been inspired today to live in the moment, in spite of fear, worries, health scares, career problems, and whatever little or big things that are weighing you down today. I hope you never forget how special this very second is.

Chapter 6:

How To Focus on Creating Positive Actions

Only a positive person can lead a healthy life. Imagine waking up every day feeling like you are ready to face the day's challenges and you are filled with hope about life. That is something an optimist doesn't have to imagine because they already feel it every day. Also, scientifically, it is proven that optimistic people have a lower chance of dying because of a stress-caused disease. Although positive thinking will not magically vanish all your problems, it will make them seem more manageable and somewhat not a big deal.

Positive thinking is what leads to positive actions, actions that affect you and the people around you. When you think positively, your actions show how positive you are. You can create positive thinking by focusing on the good in life, even if it may feel tiny thing to feel happy about because when you once learn to be satisfied with minor things, you would think that you no longer feel the same amount of stress as before and now you would feel freer. This positive attitude will always find the good in everything, and life would seem much easier than before.

Being grateful for the things you have contributed a lot to your positive behavior. Gratitude has proven to reduce stress and improve self-esteem. Think of the things you are grateful for; for example, if someone gives you good advice, then be thankful to them, for if someone has helped you with something, then be grateful to them, by being grateful about minor things, you feel more optimistic about life, you feel that good things have always been coming to you. Studies show that making down a list of things you are grateful for during hard days helps you survive through the tough times.

A person laughing always looks like a happy person. Studies have shown that laughter lowers stress, anxiety, and depression. Open yourself up to humor, permit yourself to laugh even if forced because even a forced laugh can improve your mood. Laughter lightens the mood and makes problems seem more manageable. Your laughter is contagious, and it may even enhance the perspective of the people around us.

People with depression or anxiety are always their jailers; being harsh on themselves will only cause pain, negativity, and insecurity. So try to be soft with yourself, give yourself a positive talk regularly; it has proven to affect a person's actions. A positive word to yourself can influence your ability to regulate your feelings and thoughts. The positivity you carry in your brain is expressed through your actions, and who doesn't loves an optimistic person. Instead of blaming yourself, you can think differently, like "I will do better next time" or "I can fix this." Being optimistic about the complicated situation can lead your brain to find a solution to that problem.

When you wake up, it is good to do something positive in the morning, which mentally freshens you up. You can start the day by reading a positive quote about life and understand the meaning of that quote, and you may feel an overwhelming feeling after letting the meaning set. Everybody loves a good song, so start by listening to a piece of music that gives you positive vibes, that gives you hope, and motivation for the day. You can also share your positivity by being nice to someone or doing something nice for someone; you will find that you feel thrilled and positive by making someone else happy.

Surely you can't just start thinking positively in a night, but you can learn to approach things and people with a positive outlook with some practice.

Chapter 7:
Don't Overthink Things

Analysis Paralysis, how many of you have heard of this term before? When a decision is placed before us, many of us try to weigh the pros and cons, over and over again, day and night, and never seem to be able to come up with an answer, not even one week later.

I have been guilty of doing such a thing many times in my life, in fact many in the past month alone. What I've come to realize is that there is never going to be a right decision, but that things always work out in the end as long as it is not a rash decision.

Giving careful thought to any big decision is definitely justified. From buying a car, to a house, to moving to another state or country for work, these are big life-changing decisions that could set the course for our professional and financial future for years to come. In these instances, it is okay to take as much time as we need to settle on the right calculated choice for us. Sometimes in these situations, we may not know the right answer as well but we take a leap of faith and hope for the best and that is the only thing we can do. And that is perfectly okay.

But if we translate the time and effort we take in those big projects into daily decisions such as where to go, what to eat, or who to call, we will find ourselves in a terrible predicament multiple times a day. If we overthink the simple things, life just becomes so much more complicated. We end up over-taxing our brain to the point where it does not have much juice left to do other things that are truly important.

The goal is to keep things simple by either limiting your choices or by simply going with your gut. Instead of weighing every single pro and con before making a decision, just go. The amount of time we waste calculating could be better spent into energy for other resources.

I have found that i rarely ever make a right choice even after debating hours on end whether I should go somewhere. Because i would always wonder what if i had gone to the other place instead. The human mind is very funny thing. We always seem to think the grass could be greener on the other side, and so we are never contented with what we have in front of us right here right now.

The next time you are faced with a non-life changing decision, simply flip a coin and just go with the one that the coin has chosen for you. Don't look back and flip the coin the other way unless it is truly what your heart wants. We will never be truly happy with every single choice we make. We can only make the most of it.

Chapter 8:

Everything is A Marathon Not A Sprint

Ask your parents, what was it like to raise children till the time they were able to lift their weight and be self-sufficient. I am sure they will say, it was the most beautiful experience in their lives. But believe me, They are lying.

There is no doubt in it that what you are today is because of your parents, and your parents didn't rest on their backs while a nanny was taking care of you.

They spent countless nights of sleeplessness changing diapers and soothing you so that you can have a good night's sleep. They did that because they wanted to see a part of them grow one day and become what they couldn't be. What you are today is because of their continuous struggle over the years.

You didn't grow up overnight, and your parents didn't teach you everything overnight. It took years for them to teach you and it took even more time for you to learn.

This is life!

Life is an amalgamation of little moments and each moment is more important than the last one.

Start with a small change. Learn new skills. The world around you changes every day. Don't get stuck in your routine life. Expand your horizons. What's making you money today might not even exist tomorrow. So why stick to it for the rest of your life.

You are never too old to learn new things. The day you stop learning is the last day of your life. A human being is the most supreme being in this universe for a reason. That reason is the intellect and the ability to keep moving with their lives.

You can never be a millionaire in one night. It's a one-in-billion chance to win a lottery and do that overnight. Most people see the results of their efforts in their next generation, but the efforts do pay off.

If you want to have eternal success. It will take an eternity of effort and struggles to get there. Because life is a marathon and a marathon tests your last breaths. But when it pays off, it is the highest you can get.

Shaping up a rock doesn't take one single hit, but hundreds of precision cuts with keen observation and attention. Life is that same rock, only bigger and much more difficult.

Changing your life won't happen overnight. Changing the way you see things won't happen overnight. It will take time.

To know everything and to pretend to know everything is the wrong approach to life. It's about progress. It's about learning a little bit at each step along the way.

To evolve, to adapt, to figure out things as they come, is the process of life that every living being in this universe has gone through before and will continue to go through in the future. We are who we are because of the marathon of life.

Every one of us today has more powerful things in our possessions right now than our previous 4 generations combined. So we are lucky to be in this world, in this era.

We have unlimited resources at our disposal, but we still can't get things in the blink of an eye. Because no matter how evolved we are, we still are a slave to the reality of nature, and that reality is the time itself!

If you are taking each step to expect a treat at each stop, you might not get anything. But if you believe that each step that you take is a piece in a puzzle, a puzzle that becomes a picture that is far beautiful and meaningful, believe me, the sky is your limit.

Life is a set of goals. You push and grind to get these goals but when you get there you realize that there is so much more to go on and achieve.

Committing to a goal is difficult but watching your dreams come true is something worth fighting for.

You might not see it today, you might not see it 2 years from now, but the finish line is always one step closer. Life has always been and always will be a race to the top. But only the ones who make it to the top have gone through a series of marathons and felt the grind throughout everything.

Your best is yet to come but is on the other end of that finish line.

Chapter 9:

Don't Let Eating, Sleeping, and Working Out Get In The Way of Your Productivity

From the time of Man's descend on this planet, We have literally been eating, sleeping, and working for our basic requirements.

With time and population, we did invent some things which were perfected with time as well. But in general, when you leave your teenage or enter middle age, you get into this routine of chores that only keep the cycle of life running.

The things that we take for granted today, were considered magic only a couple of hundred years ago. The feats we have done in the last fifty years may be more important and revolutionary compared to all human history. But this hasn't stopped us from seeking more.

We have two basic requirements to live; We need air to breathe and we need food to fuel up the tank. But if we start to live our lives only for those two things alone, we are no better than a prehistoric caveman.

The purpose of life is far bigger than what we perceive today.

Yeah, sometimes we get into existential crisis because we never really know what our lives mean. What the future will be and can be? What will happen at the end of all this? What was our purpose all along?

These things are natural to every sane human perception and thinking. Some people spend all their lives in search of the true meaning, in search of the truth. But the truth is that you can never know even if you have all things planned with a foolproof sketch.

But what I can tell you is that no effort goes to waste if you have a true motive. We have come too far to give up on things and leave them for others to complete. We can be satisfied with living a simple life of straightforward tasks, but we can never be fully content with our lives.

Human nature dictates us to have a second look, a second thought on even the most obvious things around us. This habit of questioning everything has brought us out of the supernatural and made us achieve things that were not even in the realm of magic.

The biggest hunger a human mind can have is the hunger for knowledge. Human beings were meant to shape up the world for the better.

Human consciousness is so vast that its limits are still unknown. So why are we still stuck on the same habits and knowledge we were born with. Why can't we ask more questions? Why can't we try to find more answers?

The only way forward for us is to keep feeding ourselves more goals and more reasons to get busy.

Life isn't just about getting up in the morning. It is about finding our true potential. It is about finding easier ways to solve problems. It is about finding bigger, better, and greater things for the generations to come.

We were given this life to inspire and be inspired. But if we have nothing new to offer to at least ourselves, what purpose are we serving then?

The Trick To Focusing

If you've been struggling with procrastinations and distractions, just not being able to do the things you know you should do and purposefully putting them off by mindlessly browsing social media or the web, then today I'm going to share with you one very simple trick that has worked for me in getting myself to focus.

I will not beat around the bush for this. The trick is to sit in silence for a minute with your work laid out in front of you in a quiet place free from noise or distractions. I know it sounds silly, but it has worked time and time again for me whenever I did this and I believe it will work the same for you.

You see our brains are constantly racing with a million thoughts. Thoughts telling us whether we should be doing our work, thoughts telling us that we should turn on the TV instead, thoughts that don't serve any real purpose but to pull us away from our goal of doing the things that matter.

Instead of being a victim of our minds, and going according to its whims and fancies. Quieting down the mind by sitting in complete silence is a good way to engage ourselves in a deeper way. A way that cuts the mind off completely, to plug ourselves out of the automated thoughts that don't serve us, and to realign ourselves with our goals and purpose of working.

To do this effectively, it is best that you turn on the AC to a comfortable temperature, sit on your working chair, lay your work out neatly in front of you, and just sit in silence for a moment. What I found that works a step up is to actually put on my noise cancelling headphones, and I find myself disappear into a clear mind. A mind free from noise, distractions, social media, music, and all the possible ways that it can throw me off my focus.

With no noise whatsoever, you will find yourself at complete peace with the world. Your thoughts about procrastination will get crushed by your feelings of serenity and peace. A feeling that you can do anything if you wanted to right now.

Everytime I turned on music or the TV, thinking I needed it as a distraction, my focus always ends up split. I operate on a much lower level of productivity because my mind is in two places. One listening to the TV or music, and the other on my work. I end up wasting more resources of my brain and end up feeling more tired and fatigued quickly than I normally would.

If that sounds familiar to you, well i have been there and done that too. And I can tell you that it is not a sustainable way to go about doing things in the long run.

The power of silence is immense. It keeps us laser focused on the task in front of us. And we hesitate less on every decision.

The next thing I would need you to do is to actually challenge yourself to be distraction free for as long as possible when you first start engaging in silence. Put all your devices on silent mode, keep it vibration free, and do not let notifications suck you back into the world of distractions. It is the number 1 killer of productivity and focus for all of us.

So if u struggle with focusing, I want you to give it a try right. If you know you are distracted there is no harm right here right now to make a choice to give this a shot.

Take out our noise cancelling earphones, turn the ac on, turn your devices off or to silent, lay your work out in front of you, turn up the lights, sit on your chair, close your eyes for a minute, and watch the magic happen.

Chapter 10:

Don't Wait Another Second To Live Your Dreams

We often think we must be ready to act , but the truth is we will never be ready while we wait.

We only become ready by walking the path, and battles are seldom won in ideal circumstances.

Money is not the real currency in life , the real currency is time and every second we wait is a second we waste.

Your biggest motivator is the ticking clock and the impending reality that one day it will be too late.

Your biggest fear is getting to 80 and realising you haven't lived, that you haven't done what you wanted in life because of fear.

True regret is a medicine none of us want to taste.

We must decide what we really want, set the bar high , go after it now and accept nothing less.

You deserve respect, but you will live what you expect, this life will pay you any price but it's up to you what you accept.

You must act now from where we are with what we have , right now , not tomorrow or next week , right now.

Take the first step , make the draft plan .

Find out what knowledge you need to make this dream a reality.

Taking action now towards the goal in mind is crucial, if we wait we risk losing the drive to make things happen.

We can never be fully ready because we don't know what exactly is going to happen, a lot of it is learned along the way - especially if you're doing something brand new.

If not, reading what has been done before in your area will give you a good understanding of what might work.

Every second we spend thinking about, instead of acting towards our goal is wasted time.

You cannot afford to wait because if you do not act , someone else will , someone else could also be thinking what you're thinking and act first.

Those who wait for opportunity will wait in vain because opportunity must be created, first in the mind, then in the world.

We cannot see the vast opportunity that surrounds us unless we believe it is there, believe it is possible and act on that belief, at the time it arises.

The world is pliable and opportunities do not wait for people to be ready.

You must become ready on the road.

The obstacles you have to overcome on the move will mould you into the person you need to be to reach your biggest goals.

You must be patient, to be practitioners of who you believe you will be one day.

Getting into the mindset of whoever you want to be right now, because until you become that person in mind, you cannot in body.

As we start acting differently, different actions bring different results and if the new actions are positive and aimed at a certain goal , just like magic the world begins to transform for you, towards the life you wanted.

The leap of faith is acting now, feeling unready aiming for something that may seem unrealistic, but this is an essential leap and test to be overcome.

As the days go on with the goal in mind , it will seem to become more likely and you will feel more ready until it feels definite.

All things are possible but there will be required ingredients to your success you might not know yet, so the first step is to gain the knowledge required.

Once you begin to learn that knowledge you are on the road to your goal.

Organization and optimization of your time will make it easier to be efficient.

If time is the real currency, are you getting good value for what you spend your time doing?

If not , is it not time you used some of your seconds working towards something phenomenal?

You only have so many and it is losing value every day as we age, think about it.

We must create a sense of urgency because it is urgent if you want to succeed in an ever changing world.

If we wait our ideas, products and services may become irrelevant because new technology and innovation is always changing.

Our ideas are only viable when they come ,

Strike while the iron is hot is good advice ,

When the ambition and goal is strongest and clearest.

Clarity is essential when pursuing dreams and goals, every detail of your dream should be clear in your mind down to the sights , colours and smells.

When we think about our goal we should feel it as if it's already here, and start acting like it is.

Dress talk and walk as if you are that person now.

Whatever our current circumstances everyone has the ability to build in their minds, set the goal then determine the first step.

If your circumstances are bad there are more steps, but there are steps.

Start from step one and walk in confidence always keeping the big dream in mind knowing that this can happen for you.

We have a waking mind and a subconscious mind.

The subconscious knows things we don't, it is responsible for our gut instinct, which always seems to be right so follow that .

Everyday listening to that voice , keeping a clear vision of your goal in your mind and confidently taking action towards it.

It's possible for you if you act ,

But time is ticking.

PART 3

Chapter 1:

Do More of What Already Works

In 2004, nine hospitals in Michigan began implementing a new procedure in their intensive care units (I.C.U.). Almost overnight, healthcare professionals were stunned by its success.

Three months after it began, the procedure had cut the infection rate of I.C.U. Patients by sixty-six percent. Within 18 months, this one method had saved 75 million dollars in healthcare expenses. Best of all, this single intervention saved the lives of more than 1,500 people in just a year and a half. The strategy was immediately published in a blockbuster paper for the New England Journal of Medicine.

This medical miracle was also simpler than you could ever imagine. It was a checklist.

This five-step checklist was the simple solution that Michigan hospitals used to save 1,500 lives. Think about that for a moment. There were no technical innovations. There were no pharmaceutical discoveries or cutting-edge procedures. The physicians just stopped skipping steps. They implemented the answers they already had on a more consistent basis.

New Solutions vs. Old Solutions

We tend to undervalue answers that we have already discovered. We underutilize old solutions—even best practices—because they seem like something we have already considered.

Here's the problem: *"Everybody already knows that"* is very different from *"Everybody already does that."* Just because a solution is known doesn't mean it is utilized.

Even more critical, just because a solution is implemented occasionally doesn't mean it is implemented consistently. Every physician knew the five steps on Peter Pronovost's checklist, but very few did all five steps flawlessly each time.

We assume that new solutions are needed to make real progress, but that isn't always the case. This pattern is just as present in our personal lives as it is in corporations and governments. We waste the resources and ideas at our fingertips because they don't seem new and exciting.

There are many examples of behaviors, big and small, that have the opportunity to drive progress in our lives if we just did them with more consistency—flossing every day—never missing workouts. Performing fundamental business tasks each day, not just when you have time—apologizing more often. Writing Thank You notes each week.

Of course, these answers are boring. Mastering the fundamentals isn't sexy, but it works. No matter what task you are working on, a simple checklist of steps you can follow right now—fundamentals that you have known about for years—can immediately yield results if you just practice them more consistently.

Progress often hides behind boring solutions and underused insights. You don't need more information. You don't need a better strategy. You just need to do more of what already works.

Chapter 2:

7 Ways To Develop Effective Communication With Your Clients

Effective communication is a significant factor in business; it is the essence of your business as clients are the core of every business. Sometimes, we forget what the client wanted; if this has happened to you, then you that your communication skills need a tad bit of improvement. The relationships you build with your clients are the key. Gaining loyal customers is essential, as they buy from you repeatedly and refer you to others, which increases customers. Communication can take many shapes and forms; it can be formal or informal and can happen over various platforms. Here are seven ways to develop practical communication skills with your clients.

1. Make It About Your Clients

When you meet someone that requires your services, you need to make it about them. It would help if you indeed gained your client's trust, but that doesn't mean the client has to hear your whole life story or several awards you have won. So whenever a new client seeks out help, remember that it is them that need help and focus on how you can impress them and meet their requirements. It is the best way to demonstrate your experience and extensive knowledge about the subject.

2. Treat Them How You'd Like To Be Treated

Business can be very tiring, sometimes when the stress is overbearing, we might feel moody and irritated but try not to take out the irritation on the clients, as your business exists because of your clients, so being rude with them will not be very wise. Try to be more patient, friendly, and positive with them, and your positive behavior shows your eagerness for your work. So try to treat your customers the most excellent way possible, the way you would want to be treated.

3. Respect Your Client's Time

"Time is money" we all have heard this famous saying, but what does it mean? The sentence gives away its meaning. It means that time is precious, whether it's yours or your clients'. Hence, try to avoid talking too much or wasting their time. Try not to make them wait for you too much that may cause unhealthiness in your relationship with your client. Try to get to the point without sounding rude or being blunt, be concise. Over media platforms, a short and well-planned consultation probably will do the work, and if they need any more information, they would ask you.

4. **Listen To Your Clients**

We all have met that annoying salesman that doesn't understand what you want or doesn't let you finish. If you have met someone like that, you know how irritating it could be, so when it is your time to be a businessman, don't do the same. When talking to your clients, please give them your undivided attention; you could do that by clearing up your brain of everything, no matter how busy the day is and how long the to-do list is. Take notes if you think you need them; try not to interrupt and stay silent if you think the customer wants to add a few more points. Listen actively to the client so that you can provide better customer service.

5. **Pay Attention To What Your Clients Say**

Any relationship requires attention; without attention, a client may seem very happy, and your business might not flourish the way you want it to. So pay attention to the tiniest of details of what the clients say. Take notes of the information that is hard to remember or seems essential. Ensure that you respond to emails, requests, or questions about your business; it will make the clients feel important. When sending out an email to your clients, double-check and see if you had made any mistakes, grammar mistakes indicate carelessness, and what kind of a client would want a careless person to help them.

6. **Actively Build Your Client Communication Skills**

If you want to create a lasting relationship with your customers, focus on your communication skills; you could set up a few rules and principles for yourself and your team to follow—brief your team on how to be friendly and provide the customer service required by the client. You can ask your client for their feedback on customer service; if they share something they don't like, you and your team can together work on that. Also, use client communication tools and software.

7. **Keep Records of Your Interactions**

Always keep records of your previous conversations with your clients; if you forgot a minor detail that was not so minor for them, it might not end pleasantly. Even the people who give clients their undivided attention forget things. So you could keep records of your interactions with your clients by making notes on a file or your mobile phone or by recording the conversation after they allow you. Making notes will also help you later, as it will help you remember who you need to check up on or follow up with.

Conclusion

Try to follow these ways, and win the trust of your clients. Be friendly and pleasant, and your clients will stay happy with you.

Chapter 3:

Be Motivated by Challenge

You have an easy life and a continuous stream of income, you are lucky! You have everything you and your children need, you are lucky! You have your whole future planned ahead of you and nothing seems to go in the other direction yet, you are lucky!

But how far do you think this can go? What surety can you give yourself that all will go well from the start to the very end?

Life will always have a hurdle, a hardship, a challenge, right there when you feel most satisfied. What will you do then?

Will you give up and look for an escape? Will you seek guidance? Or will you just give up and go down a dark place because you never thought something like this could happen to you?

Life is full of endless possibilities and an endless parade of challenges that make life no walk in the park.

You are different from any other human being in at least one attribute. But your life isn't much different than most people's. You may be less fortunate or you may be the luckiest, but you must not back down when life strikes you.

This world is a cruel place and a harsh terrain. But that doesn't mean you should give up whenever you get hit in the back. That doesn't mean you don't catch what the world throws at you.

Do you know what you should do? Look around and observe for examples. Examples of people who have had the same experiences as you had and what good or bad things did they do? You will find people on both extremes.

You will find people who didn't have the courage or guts to stand up to the challenge and people who didn't have the time to give up but to keep pushing harder and harder, just to get better at what they failed the last time.

The challenges of life can never cross your limits because the limits of a human being are practically infinite. But what feels like a heavy load, is just a shadow of your inner fear dictating you to give up.

But you can't give up, right? Because you already have what you need to overcome this challenge too. You just haven't looked into your backpack of skills yet!

If you are struggling at college, go out there and prove everyone in their wrong. Try to get better grades by putting in more hours little by little.

If people take you as a non-social person, try to talk to at least one new person each day.

If you aren't getting good at a sport, get tutorials and try to replicate the professionals step by step and put in all your effort and time if you truly care for the challenge at hand.

The motivation you need is in the challenge itself. You just need to realize the true gains you want from each stone in your path and you will find treasures under every stone.

Chapter 4:

Becoming High Achievers

By becoming high achievers we become high off life, what better feeling is there than aiming for something you thought was unrealistic and then actually hitting that goal. What better feeling is there than declaring we will do something against the perceived odds and then actually doing it.

To be a high achiever you must be a believer,

You must believe in yourself and believe that dream is possible for you.

It doesn't matter what anyone else thinks , as long as you believe,

To be a high achiever we must hunger to achieve.

To be an action taker.

Moving forward no matter what.

High achievers do not quit.

Keeping that vision in their minds eye until it becomes reality, no matter what.

Your biggest dream is protected by fear , loss and pain.

We must conquer all 3 of these impostors to walk through the door.

Not many do , most are still fighting fear and if they lose the battle, they quit.

Loss and pain are part of life.

Losses are hard on all of us.

Whether we lose possessions, whether we lose friends, whether we lose our jobs, or whether we lose family members.

Losing doesn't mean you have lost.

Losses are may be a tough pill to swallow, but they are essential because we cannot truly succeed until we fail.

We can't have the perfect relationship if we stay in a toxic one, and we can't have the life we desire until we make room by letting go of the old.

The 3 imposters that cause us so much terror are actually the first signs of our success. So walk through fear in courage , look at loss as an eventual gain, and know that the pain is part of the game and without it you would be weak.

Becoming a high achiever requires a single minded focus on your goal, full commitment and an unnatural amount of persistence and work.

We must define what high achievement means to us individually, set the bar high and accept nothing less.

The achievement should not be money as money is not our currency but a tool.

The real currency is time and your result is the time you get to experience the world's places and products , so the result should always be that.

The holiday home , the fast car and the lifestyle of being healthy and wealthy, those are merely motivations to work towards. Like Carrots on a stick.

High achievement is individual to all of us, it means different things to each of us,

But if we are going to go for it we might as well go all out for the life we want, should we not?

I don't think we beat the odds of 1 in 400 trillion to be born, just to settle for mediocrity, did we?

Being a high achiever is in your DNA , if you can beat the odds , you can beat anything. It is all about self-belief and confidence, we must have the confidence to take the action required and often the risk.

Risk is difficult for people and it's a difficult tight rope to walk. The line between risk and recklessness is razor thin.

Taking risks feels unnatural, not surprisingly as we all grew up in a health and safety bubble with all advice pointing towards safe and secure ways.

But the reward is often in the risk and sometimes a leap of blind faith is required. This is what stops most of us - the fear of the unknown.

The truth is the path to success is foggy and we can only ever see one step ahead , we have to imagine the result and know it's somewhere down this foggy path and keep moving forward with our new life in mind.

Know that we can make it but be aware that along the path we will be met by fear , loss and pain and the bigger our goal the bigger these monsters will be.

The top achievers financially are fanatical about their work and often work 100+ hours per week.

Some often work day and night until a project is successful.

Being a high achiever requires giving more than what is expected, standing out for the high standard of your work because being known as number 1 in your field will pay you abundantly.

Being an innovator, thinking outside the box for better practices, creating superior products to your competition because quality is more rewarding than quantity.

Maximizing the quality of your products and services to give assurance to your customers that your company is the number 1 choice.

What can we do differently to bring a better result to the table and a better experience for our customers?

We must think about questions like that because change is inevitable and without thinking like that we get left behind, but if we keep asking that, we can successfully ride the wave of change straight to the beach of our desired results.

The route to your success is by making people happy because none of us can do anything alone, we must earn the money and to earn it we must make either our employers or employees and customers happy.

To engage in self-promotion and positive interaction with those around us, we must be polite and positive with everyone, even with our competition.

Because really the only competition is ourselves and that is all we should focus on.

Self-mastery, how can I do better than yesterday?

What can I do different today that will improve my circumstances for tomorrow.

Little changes add up to a big one.

The belief and persistence towards your desired results should be 100%, I will carry on until… is the right attitude.

We must declare to ourselves that we will do this , we don't yet know how but we know that we will.

Because high achievers like yourselves know that to make it you must endure and persist untill you win.

High achievers have an unnatural grit and thick skin , often doing what others won't, putting in the extra hours when others don't.

After you endure loss and conquer pain , the sky is the limit, and high achievers never settle until they are finished.

Chapter 5:
The Struggle With Time

Today we're going to talk about a topic that isn't commonly looked at in depth. But it is one that we might hopefully find a new appreciation for. And that is TIME.

Time is a funny thing, we are never really aware of it and how much of a limited resource it really is until we get a rude awakening. Most commonly when our mortality is tested. Whether it be a health scare, an accident, a death of a loved one, a death of a pet, we always think we have more time before that. That we will always have time to say i love you, to put off the things we always told ourselves we needed to do, to start making that change, to spend time with the people that mean the most to us.

As we go about our days, weeks and months, being bothered and distracted by petty work, by our bosses, colleagues, trying to climb the corporate ladder, we forget to stop and check in on our fiends and family... We forget that their time may be running out, and that we may not have as much time with them as we think we do, until it is too late, and then we regret not prioritising them first. All the money that we made could not ever buy back the time we have lost with them. And that is something we have to live with if we ever let that happen.

The other funny thing about time is that if we don't set it aside for specific tasks, if we don't schedule anything, we will end up wasting it on something mindless. Whether it be browsing social media endlessly, or bingeing on television, we will never run out of things to fill that time with. Can you imagine that even though time is so precious, we willingly sacrifice and trade it in for self isolation in front of our TVs and computers for hours on end. Sometimes even for days? Or even on mobile games. Some being so addictive that it consumes most of our waking hours if we are not careful.

Our devices have become dangerous time wasters. It is a tool Shea its literally sapping the living energy out of us. Which is why some responsible companies have started implementing new features that help us keep track of our screen time. To keep us in check, and to not let our children get sucked into this black hole that we might struggle to climb out of.

I believe the biggest struggle with time that we all have is how to spend it in such a way that we can be happy without feeling guilty. Guilty of not spending it wisely. And I believe the best way to start is to start defining the things that you need to do, and the things that you want to do. And then striking a balance. To set equal amounts of time into each activity so that it doesn't overwhelm or underwhelm you. Spend one hour on each activity each day that you feel will have an impact on your life in a meaningful way, and you can spend your time on television or games without remorse.

So I challenge each of you to make the most of your time. SPending time with loved ones always come first, followed by your goals and dreams, and then leisure activities. Never the other way around. That way you can be at the end of your life knowing that you had not wasted the most precious commodity that we are only given a finite amount of. Money can't buy back your youth, your health, or time with loved ones, so don't waste it.

I believe in each and everyone of you, take care, and as always ill see you in the next one.

Chapter 6:

6 Reasons Your Emotions Are Getting In The Way Of Your Success

Do you ever ponder on why your new year's resolutions fail miserably? It is primarily because of the toxic emotions and our negative thoughts of the past that keeps us stuck with the same patterns and regrets. We can try to change and manage our attitudes well, but the emotions are out of our hands. So even though we can't control what we feel, we must confront them to achieve our goals and resolutions.

A therapist in Tarzana, California, Vicki Botnick, explains that any emotion – even elation, joy, or others you would typically view as positive – can intensify to a point where it becomes difficult to control.

Here are 6 Reasons why emotions are getting in the way of your success

1. You let your emotions rule you

Most of us are clueless about taking control of our emotions and how they affect our productivity. But we must manage them if we strive to achieve our goals. Emotions are an instant response to a specific trigger. All of our emotions are interlinked with each other. For example, we can't taste the satisfaction of joy if we don't go through any pain, or we can't enjoy courage without being fearful first. All of these emotions are what make us human. Embracing both negative and positive emotions are essential, but if they start to get in the way of your success, then you must take action and act upon them.

2. Anger.

"The greatest remedy for anger is a delay." - Thomas Paine.

Anger is the majorly common emotion that humankind feels. This negative emotion can result from frustrations, conflicts, mistreatment, or interpersonal conflicts, or is sometimes triggered by an event or experience that happened in the past. For example, suppose you studied really hard for a test but didn't get the expected grade. The next time when you're willing to give it another try, you won't study as much as you did the first time because you'll remember your previous failed attempt. You will re-live your failure and will eventually become frustrated and demotivated. The best thing to do in this scenario is just to take some time off and breathe. Distance yourself from everything and get yourself to calm down before making any decision. Ask yourself then, are you too hard on yourself? Are you trying to do everything at once that's causing you to get upset? Have you set the bar too high? Ponder on these questions and then look for the solutions calmly. Being angry about the things you can't control is pointless, as anger feeds more anger, and you would get stuck in an endless loop of resentment and frustration. Seek solutions on the things you can control and be patient.

3. Fear.

The fear of failure is perhaps the worst emotion we can endure. It snatches away even the slightest chance of taking that first step to achieving our dreams and goals. The reasons why we are so afraid of failures may vary from person to person. Some people can't digest that they are full of flaws and that failure is the most crucial step towards leading a successful life. They want to win no matter what. Others might feel that they are not good enough if they can't achieve something. Most people don't admit that they have fears. Fear can either be your greatest friend or your worst enemy; it all depends on how you treat it, whether you look into its eyes and face it or run from it. Living fearlessly doesn't mean that a person isn't afraid of anything, but rather that the person has befriended his fears and is now dancing with them. One shouldn't run away from the challenges that the world throws at him, but stand up to them bravely and face them. Make a list of all the things that scare you or are distracting you from achieving your goals. And then work towards them until they no longer bother you or gets in the way of your success. A famous African proverb states, "Smooth seas do not make skillful sailors."

4. Envy.

Bertrand Russell once said, "Beggars do not envy millionaires, though of course, they will envy other beggars who are more successful." Envy and jealousy are the two strongest emotions that mankind has experienced. Although they go hand in hand with each other, there is still a slight difference between them. Being envious wants the other person's things, while jealousy wants the other person's recognition from others. Whenever things tend to go south, we start to become envious of those who are successful. We compare ourselves to them, idealize their successes, and in the process, we lose ourselves. We shift our focus from our signs of progress to being demotivated and stressed out. Pain is an indicator of progress. When we stretch our minds beyond our comfort zone, we feel pain. This pain is the indication that we should move forward and not run away. We shouldn't compare our initial progress to those who have been striving for years. Everyone has their own pace. We should focus on ourselves and setting our potentials free.

5. **Guilt.**

The guilt of doing something else or saying something else instead of what you already did or said will forever haunt us. Guilt gets us stuck in the past rather than live in the present moment. There is a term in psychology, The Zeigarnik Effect, which refers that people remember uncompleted tasks more than the completed ones. They then blame themselves for not doing it sooner or better. Our mindset is often linked with productivity blame, where we feel bad for achieving something or not working hard enough. We tend to punish ourselves emotionally and get the idea that we can never reach our goals. But it is essential to take some time off and treat yourself with kindness and empathy. Don't over-pressurize yourself. Self-appreciate and become a better version of yourself in the process. "Mistakes are always forgivable if one dares to admit them." - Bruce Lee.

6. **Sadness.**

"We must understand that sadness is an ocean, and sometimes we drown, while other days, we are forced to swim." - R.M. Drake.

Feeling sad or low on energy crushes productivity and enthusiasm. We feel demotivated and can't focus on our tasks. Sadness makes us feel secluded and isolated. We must embrace this emotion at our own pace, but we shouldn't hide away from whatever it is that's bothering us. Start again slowly with your productivity, make slight progress, start rechallenging yourself. But don't do all of this unless you feel okay again.

Conclusion:

Understanding how your emotions are getting in the way of your productivity requires practice. Self-awareness is the key to know yourself better, so you can deal with your emotions efficiently. Please pay close attention to what your feelings are trying to tell you rather than running away from them.

Chapter 7:

5 Tips for A More Creative Brain

Nearly all great ideas follow a similar creative process, and this article explains how this process works. Understanding this is important because creative thinking is one of the most useful skills you can possess. Nearly every problem you face in work and life can benefit from creative solutions, lateral thinking, and innovative ideas.

Anyone can learn to be creative by using these five steps. That's not to say being creative is easy. Uncovering your creative genius requires courage and tons of practice. However, this five-step approach should help demystify the creative process and illuminate the path to more innovative thinking.

To explain how this process works, let me tell you a short story.

A Problem in Need of a Creative Solution

In the 1870s, newspapers, and printers faced a very specific and very costly problem. Photography was a new and exciting medium at the time.

Readers wanted to see more pictures, but nobody could figure out how to print images quickly and cheaply.

For example, if a newspaper wanted to print an image in the 1870s, they had to commission an engraver to etch a copy of the photograph onto a steel plate by hand. These plates were used to press the image onto the page, but they often broke after a few uses. This process of photoengraving, you can imagine, was remarkably time-consuming and expensive.

The man who invented a solution to this problem was named Frederic Eugene Ives. He became a trailblazer in the field of photography and held over 70 patents by the end of his career. His story of creativity and innovation, which I will share now, is a useful case study for understanding the five key steps of the creative process.

A Flash of Insight

Ives got his start as a printer's apprentice in Ithaca, New York. After two years of learning the ins and outs of the printing process, he began managing the photographic laboratory at nearby Cornell University. He spent the rest of the decade experimenting with new photography techniques and learning about cameras, printers, and optics.

In 1881, Ives had a flash of insight regarding a better printing technique.

"While operating my photo stereotypes process in Ithaca, I studied the problem of the halftone process," Ives said. "I went to bed one night in a state of brain fog over the problem, and the instant I woke in the morning saw before me, apparently projected on the ceiling, the completely worked out process and equipment in operation."

Ives quickly translated his vision into reality and patented his printing approach in 1881. He spent the remainder of the decade improving upon it. By 1885, he had developed a simplified process that delivered even better results. As it came to be known, the Ives Process reduced the cost of printing images by 15x and remained the standard printing technique for the next 80 years.

Alright, now let's discuss what lessons we can learn from Ives about the creative process.

The 5 Stages of the Creative Process

In 1940, an advertising executive named James Webb Young published a short guide titled, A Technique for Producing Ideas. In this guide, he made a simple but profound statement about generating creative ideas.

According to Young, innovative ideas happen when you develop new combinations of old elements. In other words, creative thinking is not about generating something new from a blank slate but rather about taking what is already present and combining those bits and pieces in a way that has not been done previously.

Most importantly, generating new combinations hinges upon your ability to see the relationships between concepts. If you can form a new link between two old ideas, you have done something creative.

Young believed this process of creative connection always occurred in five steps.

1. **Gather new material.** At first, you learn. During this stage, you focus on 1) learning specific material directly related to your task and 2) learning general material by becoming fascinated with a wide range of concepts.

2. **Thoroughly work over the materials in your mind.** During this stage, you examine what you have learned by looking at the facts from different angles and experimenting with fitting various ideas together.

3. **Step away from the problem.** Next, you put the problem completely out of your mind and do something else that excites you and energizes you.

4. **Let your idea return to you.** At some point, but only after you stop thinking about it will your idea come back to you with a flash of insight and renewed energy.

5. **Shape and develop your idea based on feedback.** For any idea to succeed, you must release it out into the world, submit it to criticism, and adapt it as needed.

Chapter 8:

Develop A Habit of Studying

Life is a series of lessons.

Your education does not end at 16 or 18 or 21,

It has only just begun.

You are a student of life.

You are constantly learning, whether you know it or not.

You have a free will of what you learn and which direction you go.

If you develop a habit of studying areas of personal interest,

your life will head in the direction of your interests.

If you study nothing you will be forced to learn and change through

tragedy and negative circumstances.

What you concentrate on you become,

so study and concentrate on something that you want.

If you study a subject for just one hour per day, in a year you would of

studied 365 hours, making you a national expert.

If you keep it up for 5 years, that's 1825 hours , making you an

international expert, all from one hour per day.

If you commit to two hours you will half that time.

Studying is the yellow brick road to your dream life.

Through concentration and learning you will create that life.

Knowledge opens doors.

Being recognised as an expert increases pay.

Not studying keeps you were you are –

Closed doors and a stagnant income.

If you don't learn anything how can you expect to be valuable?

If you don't grow how can you expect to be paid more?

It only becomes too late to learn when you are dead;

until then the world is an open book will billions of pages.

Often what we deem impossible is in fact possible.

Often even your most lofty dreams you haven't even scratched the

surface of what you are capable of.

Taylor your study to your goal –

follow the yellow brick road of your design.

Follow the road you have built and walk toward your goals.

If you want to be successful, study success and successful people,

then learn everything you can about your chosen field.

Plan your day with a set time for your study.

I don't care how busy you claim to be,

everybody can spare 1 hour out of 24 to work on themselves.

If not , I hope you're happy where you are,

because that is about as far as you will get without learning more.

Studying is crucial to success whether it's formal

or learning from books and online material at home.

The knowledge you learn will progress you towards your dream life.

If that is not worth an hour or two per day,

then maybe you don't want it enough and that's ok.

Maybe you want something different to what you thought,

or maybe you're happy where you are.

If not, it's on you to do this –

for yourself,

for your family,

and for your partner in life.

It's up to you to create the world you want –

A world that only you know if you deserve.

You must learn the knowledge and build the dream

because the world needs your creation.

Be a keen student of life and apply its lesson

to build your future on a solid and safe foundation.

Chapter 9:
6 Steps To Get Out of Your Comfort Zone

The year 2020 and 2021 have made a drastic change in all our lives, which might have its effect forever. The conditions of last year and a half have made a certain lifestyle choice for everyone, without having a say in it for us.

This new lifestyle has been a bit overwhelming for some and some started feeling lucky. Most of us feel comfortable working from home, and taking online classes while others want to have some access to public places like parks and restaurants.

But the pandemic has affected everyone more than once. And now we are all getting used to this relatively new experience of doing everything from home. Getting up every day to the same routine and the same environment sometimes takes us way back on our physical and mental development and creativity.

So one must learn to leave the comfort zone and keep themselves proactive. Here are some ways anyone can become more productive and efficient.

Everyone is always getting ready to change but never changing.

1. Remember your Teenage Self

People often feel nostalgic remembering those days of carelessness when they were kids and so oblivious in that teenage. But, little do they take for inspiration or motivation from those times. When you feel down, or when you don't feel like having the energy for something, just consider your teenage self at that time.

If only you were a teenager now, you won't be feeling lethargic or less motivated. Rather you'd be pushing harder and harder every second to get the job done as quickly as possible. If you could do it back then, you still can! All you need is some perspective and a medium to compare to.

2. Delegate or Mentor someone

Have you ever needed to have someone who could provide you some guidance or help with a problem that you have had for some time?

I'm sure, you weren't always a self-made man or a woman. Somewhere along the way, there was someone who gave you the golden quote that changed you consciously or subconsciously.

Now is the time for you to do the same for someone else. You could be a teacher, a speaker, or even a mentor who doesn't have any favors to ask in return. Once you get the real taste of soothing someone else's pain, you won't hesitate the next time.

This feeling of righteousness creates a chain reaction that always pushes you to get up and do good for anyone who could need you.

3. Volunteer in groups

The work of volunteering may seem pointless or philanthropic. But the purpose for you to do it should be the respect that you might get, but the stride to get up on your feet and help others to be better off.

Volunteering for flood victims, earthquake affectees or the starving people of deserts and alpines can help you understand the better purpose of your existence. This keeps the engine of life running.

4. Try New Things for a Change

Remember the time in Pre-school when your teachers got you to try drawing, singing, acting, sculpting, sketching, and costume parties. Those weren't some childish approach to keep you engaged, but a planned system to get your real talents and skills to come out.

We are never too old to learn something new. Our passions are unlimited just as our dreams are. We only need a push to keep discovering the new horizons of our creative selves.

New things lead to new people who lead to new places which might lead to new possibilities. This is the circle of life and life is ironic enough to rarely repeat the same thing again.

You never know which stone might lead you to a gold mine. So never stop discovering and experiencing because this is what makes us the supreme being.

5. Push Your Physical Limits

This may sound cliched, but it always is the most important point of them all. You can never get out of your comfort zone, till you see the world through the hard glass.

The world is always softer on one side, but the image on the other side is far from reality. You can't expect to get paid equally to the person who works 12 hours a day in a large office of hundreds of employees. Only if you have the luxury of being the boss of the office.

You must push yourself to search for opportunities at every corner. Life has always more and better to offer at each stop, you just have to choose a stop.

6. Face Your Fears Once and For All

People seem to have a list of Dos and Dont's. The latter part is mostly because of a fear or a vacant thought that it might lead to failure for several reasons.

You need a "Do it all" behavior in life to have an optimistic approach to everything that comes in your way.

What is the biggest most horrible thing that can happen if you do any one of these things on your list? You need to have a clear vision of the possible worst outcome.

If you have a clear image of what you might lose, now must try to go for that thing and remove your fear once and for all. Unless you have something as important as your life to lose, you have nothing to fear from anything.

No one can force you to directly go skydiving if you are scared of heights. But you can start with baby steps, and then, maybe, later on in life you dare to take a leap of faith.

"Life is a rainbow, you might like one color and hate the other. But that doesn't make it ugly, only less tempting".

All you need is to be patient and content with what you have today, here, right now. But, you should never stop aiming for more. And you certainly shouldn't regret it if you can't have or don't have it now.

People try to find their week spots and frown upon those moments of hard luck. What they don't realize is, that the time they wasted crying for what is in the past, could have been well spent for a far better future they could cherish for generations to come.

Chapter 10:

Don't Make Life Harder Than It Needs To Be

Today we're going to talk about a topic that I hope will inspire you to make better decisions and to take things more lightly. As we go through this journey of life together, and as we get older, we soon find ourselves with more challenges that we need to face, more problems that we need to solve, and more responsibilities that we need to take on as an adult. In each phase of life, the bar gets set higher for us. When we are young, our troubles mostly revolve around school and education. For most of us we don't have to worry much about making money or trying to provide for a family, although I know that some of you who come from lesser well off families might have had to start doing a lot earlier. And to you i commend you greatly. For the rest of us we deal with problems with early teenage dating, body image, puberty, grades, and so on. It is only until we graduate from university do we face the harsh reality of the real world. Of being a working adult. It is only then are we really forced to grow up. To face nasty colleagues, bosses, customers, you name it. And that is only just the beginning.

Life starts to get more complicated for many of us when we start to realise that we have to manage our own finances now. When our parents stop giving us money and that we only have ourselves to rely on to survive. Suddenly reality hits us like a truck. We realise that making our own money becomes our primary focus and that we may not have much else to rely on. We take on loans, mortgages, credit card debts, and it seems to never really end. For many of us, we may end up in a rat race that we can't get out of because of the payments and loans that we have already ended up committing to. The things we buy have a direct impact on the obligations that have to maintain.

Next we have to worry about finding a partner, marriage, starting a family, buying a house, providing for your kids, setting aside money for their growth, college fund, the list goes on and on.

Do you feel overwhelmed with this summary of the first maybe one-third of your life? The reality is that that is probably the exact time line that most of us will eventually go through. The next phase of life requires us to keep up the payments, to go to our jobs, to keep making that dough to sustain our family. We may have to also make enough money to pay for tuition fees, holidays, gifts, payments to parents, and whatever other commitments that we might have. And this might go on until we reach 60, when two-thirds of our lives are already behind us.

Life as you can see, without any external help, is already complicated enough. If you didn't already know by now, life isn't easy. Life is full of challenges, obligations, obstacles, commitments, and this is without any unforeseen events that might happen... Medical or family wise.

With all this in mind, why do we want to make life harder than it already is?

Every additional decision that you make on top of this list will only add to your burden, if it is not the right one, and every person that you add into your life that is negative will only bring the experience much less enjoyable.

To make life easier for you and your soul, I recommend that you choose each step wisely. Choose carefully the partner that you intend to spend your life with, choose wisely the people that you choose to spend your time with, choose wisely the food that you put in your body, and choose wisely the life that you wish to lead.

Be absolutely clear on the vision that you have for your life because it ain't easy.

Another thing to make your life much less complicated is to put less pressure on yourself. I believe that you don't need to start comparing your life with others because everyone is on their own journey. Don't chase the fancy houses and cars that your friends have just because they have them. Everyone is different and everyone's priorities might be different as well. They might pride having a luxury car over spending on other areas of life, which might differ from the interests that you might have. Comparison will only most certainly lead you to chase a life that you might not even want to attain. And you might lose your sleep and mind trying to match up to your peers. Focus on yourself instead and on exactly what you want out of life and it will definitely be enough.

I challenge each and everyone of you to have a clear set of priorities for yourself. And once you have done so and are working towards those goals, be contented about it. Don't change the goalpost just because your friends say you must, or because you are jealous of what they have. Be satisfied in your own path and life will reward you with happiness as well.

I hope you learned something today. Thank you and I'll see you in the next one.

7 Ways To Discover Your Strengths

It is a fact that everybody has at least one skill, one talent, and one gift that is unique to them only. Everyone has their own set of strengths and weaknesses. Helen Keller was blind but her talent of speaking moved the world. Stephen Hawking theorised the genesis by sitting paralyzed in a wheelchair. The barber who does your hair must have a gifted hand for setting YOUR hair at reasonable prices—otherwise you wouldn't be visiting them.

See, the thing is, everyone is a prodigy at one thing or another. It's only waiting to be discovered and harnessed. Keeping that fact in mind…

Here are 7 Ways You can Discover Your Potential Strengths and Change Your Life Forever:

1. Try Doing Things That You Have Never Done

Imagine what would have happened if Elvis Presley never tried singing, if Michael Jordan never tried playing basketball or if Mark Zuckerberg never tried coding. These individuals would have been completely different persons, serving different purposes in life. Even the whole world would've been different today if some specific people didn't try doing some specific things in their lives.

Unfortunately, many of us never get to know what we are truly good at only because we don't choose to do new things. We don't feel the need to try and explore things that we have never done before in our lives. As a result, our gifted talents remain undiscovered and many of us die with it. So while the time is high, do as many different things you can and see what suits you naturally. That is how you can discover your talent and afterwards, it's only a matter of time before you put it to good use and see your life change dramatically.

2.   Don't Get Too Comfortable With Your Current State

It is often the case that we cling on to our current state of being and feel absolutely comfortable in doing so. In some cases, people may even embrace the job that they don't like doing only because 'it pays enough'. And honestly, I totally respect their point of view, it's up to people what makes them happy. But if you ask me how one can discover their hidden talents—how one might distinguish oneself—then I'm going to have to say that never get used to doing one particular thing. If one job or activity occupies you so much that you can't even think of something else, then you can never go out to venture about doing new stuff. The key is to get out, or should I say 'break out' from what you are doing right now and move on to the next thing. What is the next thing you might want to try doing before you die? Life is short, you don't want to go on your whole life, never having experienced something out of your comfort bubble.

3.   What Is The Easiest Thing You Can Do?

Have you ever found yourself in a place where you did something for the first time and immediately you stood out from the others? If yes, then chances are, that thing might be one of your natural strengths.

If you've seen 'Forrest Gump', you should remember the scene where Forrest plays table-tennis for the first time in a hospital and he's just perfect at the game. "For some reason, ping-pong came very naturally to me, so I started playing it all the time. I played ping-pong even when I didn't have anyone to play ping-pong with.", says Forrest in the movie.

So bottomline, pay attention to it if something comes about being 'too easy' for you. Who knows, you might be the world's best at it.

4. Take Self-Assessment Tests

There are countless, free self-assessment tests that are available online in all different kinds of formats. Just google it and take as many tests you like. Some of these are just plain and general aptitude tests or IQ tests, personality tests etc. while there are others which are more particular and tell you what type of job is suited for you, what kind of skills you might have, what you might be good at, and those kinds of things. These tests are nothing but a number of carefully scripted questions which reveal a certain result based on how you answered each question. A typical quiz wouldn't take more than 30 minutes while there are some short and long quizzes which might take 15 minutes and 45 minutes respectively.

Though the results are not very accurate, it can do a pretty good job at giving you a comprehensive, shallow idea of who you are and what you can be good at.

5.   Make Notes On How You Deal With Your Problems

Everyone faces difficult situations and overcomes them in one way or the other. That's just life. You have problems, you deal with them, you move on and repeat.

But trouble comes in all shapes and sizes and with that, you are forced to explore your problem-solving skills—you change your strategies and tactics—and while at it, sometimes you do things that are extraordinary for you, without even realizing it. John Pemberton was trying out a way to solve his headache problem using Coca leaves and Kola nuts, but incidentally he made the world's coke-drink without even knowing about it. Lesson to be learned, see how YOU deal with certain problems and why is it different from the others who are trying to solve the same problem as you.

6.   Ask Your Closest Friends and Family

People who spend a lot of time with you, whether it be your friend, family or even a colleague gets to see you closely, how you work, how you behave, how you function overall. They know what kind of a person you are and at one point, they can see through you in a manner that you yourself never can. So, go ahead and talk to them, ask them what THEY think your strongest suit can be—listen to them, try doing what they think you might turn out to be really good at, Who knows?

7.   Challenge Yourself

The growth of a human being directly corresponds to the amount of challenge a person faces from time to time. The more a person struggles, the more he or she grows—unlocks newer sets of skills and strengths. This is a lifelong process and there's no limit on how far you can go, how high your talents can accomplish.

Now, one might say, "what if I don't have to struggle too much? What if my life is going easy on me?". For them, I'd say "invite trouble". Because if you are eager to know about your skills and strengths (I assume you are since you're reading this), you must make yourself face difficulties and grow from those experiences. Each challenge you encounter and overcome redefines your total strength.

Final Thoughts

To sum it up, your life is in your hands, under your control. But life is short and you gotta move fast. Stop pursuing what you are not supposed to do and set out to find your natural talents RIGHT NOW. Once you get to know your strengths, you will have met your purpose in life.